THE GOLDEN BOOK OF
AMSTERDAM

220 Colour illustrations

BONECHI

* * *

© Copyright by
Casa Editrice Bonechi
Via Cairoli 18/b, Florence - Italy
Telex 571323 CEB - Fax (55)5000766

ISBN 88-7009-602-5

Translation: Studio COMUNICARE, Florence

Printed in Italy by
CENTRO STAMPA EDITORIALE BONECHI
Florence

*The photographs are the property of the archives of the
Casa Editrice Bonechi and were taken by:
Ronald Glaudemans, Joop ten Veen, Paolo Giambone,
Andrea Pistolesi, Marco Banti.*

*The photographs on page 10 (below) were kindly provided
by the Stichting Koninklijk Paleis, Amsterdam.*

*The photographs on pages 70, 71, 72, 74, 75 were kindly
provided by the Rijksmuseum-Stichting, Amsterdam.*

*The photographs on pages 78, 79, 80, 81, 82 were kindly
provided by Photo Service - Gruppo Editoriale Fabbri.*

*The photographs on page 5 (Lemcke), page 51 (below) (H.
van den Leeden) and page 109 (G. Wetten) were kindly
provided by the Nederlands Bureau voor Toerisme.*

The picturesque houses that flank the Oudezijds Voorburgwal.

THE HISTORY OF AMSTERDAM

Practically nothing is known about Amsterdam's history in the prehistoric and Roman periods: it is not until the Middle Ages that the name of the city appears for the first time in an official document. However, there is a legend about its foundation, according to which two fishermen, surprised by a violent storm while fishing at sea with their dog, were shipwrecked and built a refuge in the swamps, where the River Amstel flows into the estuary of the Zuider Zee, also called the IJ. This settlement, founded by the two fishermen and their families who joined them later, is said to be the origin of what was to be Amsterdam. They built a village at the mouth of the Amstel River and also made a dam to protect their homes from the stormy waters. This was the derivation of the city's name, Amstelledamme (dam
on the Amstel), which later became Amsterdam. The city is mentioned by its earlier name for the first time in a charter dated 27 October 1275, in which a feudal lord, Floris V, Count of Holland, guarantees exemption from taxes and the right of free trade to its inhabitants: «homines manentes apud Amstelledamme». Amstelledamme grew up along the banks of the Amstel and from its very beginnings learnt to live on and draw its livelihood from water. Its fortunate geographical position and the hard work of its people meant that the simple fishing village became a large trading centre, with an extremely important port and flourishing trade with the Baltic and the Mediterranean basin. At the beginning of the 17th century, this sea trade reached new and even grander heights. After the fall of its rival port of

3

Vivid reflections on a canal.

Antwerp, opposed by the might of Spain, Amsterdam virtually became the mistress of the seas, and this was the beginning of what is rightly known as the Golden Age of Holland. Welcoming the cultural and ideological contribution of exiles fleeing from the Inquisition, who found here a tolerant refuge where they were permitted to publish their philosophical and political works and were free to practise their Protestant religion, Amsterdam became a great world power. This was the era of the burgeoning trade in tea, tobacco, cocoa, diamonds (the Amsterdammers became expert diamond cutters), coffee, rubber and spices; it was the era in which the famous West India and East India Companies were founded; and it was the era in which the three great concentric canals were built in Amsterdam and along them the splendid dwellings of the city's richest and most aristocratic citizens. The merchant was the protagonist in the life of Amsterdam in this period; and it uas he who built the long rows of narrow houses, because the city's building taxes were based on house frontage. But Amsterdam's role as a great power was not destined to last long. Nearby England, which rivalled her for the dominion of the seas, soon learned to construct lighter and faster ships. And as English and French power grew, the strength of Amsterdam was gradually sapped, until in 1795 Dutch soil was occupied by Dutch patriots; they set up the Batavian Republic, and the Dutch king, William V of Orange, fled to England. The republic did not last long since in 1806 it was replaced by the rule of Napoleon Bonaparte. In 1813 Amsterdam was the first city in Holland to rebel against the French invaders, heading the movement which eventually led to the founding of an independent kingdom. Finally, the long years during which Amsterdam and Holland succeeded in maintaining their neutrality came to an end in 1940 with the occupation by the Nazi army. Only five years later was Amsterdam to become a free city again.
The centuries of Amsterdam's greatness left their indlible mark. The canals, bridges, mansions and simpler houses which we can still see today in the old centre of Amsterdam are the ones dating from the golden era which began in the 17th century, wisely and carefully preserved by the inhabitants of Amsterdam.

Airview over Dam.

THE DAM

It is the most famous square in Holland. The fishing village which was later transformed into Amsterdam was built right on this very spot in about 1270. It is the ideal city centre, even if it ceased to be the geographic heart and administrative seat years ago. Right throughout the sixties, hippies and Provos from all over Europe met at the Dam. Only during the day does the square continue to teem with young people and visitors from all over the world.

They sit on the white steps of the National Monument, a favourite, historic meeting place.

It is the Dam that gave the city its name. In this square the Waterlanders, who originally lived in the North on the sea, built the dyke, which is the Dutch word for dam, blocking the flow of the Amstel and separating it from the IJ, a wide arm of the Zuidersee. The Waterlanders were looking for rich, fertile land to serve also as a barrier. They landed on the sandy banks of the mouth of the Amstel, and to protect themselves against the tides and recurring flooding on the river,

they built this initial dyke which constituted their quick fortune. In short, the Dam became the space in which the entire community met for official ceremonies and the most important events, a deeprooted habit still maintained by Amsterdam's townsfolk. In the Middle Ages the Dam faced the sea, from where ships set sail for the North Sea. Today the end part of the Amstel has completely disappeared, its flow having been deviated: its mouth has been silted up between the Damrak and Rokin, the two main channels of communication which cross the Dam, cutting it in half.

THE MONUMENT
TO THE LIBERATION

The imposing white obelisk decorated with allegorical figures was put up by J. Radeker in 1956 in eternal remembrance of the Dutch victims of World War II. The monument encompasses twelve urns, each of which contains a handful of earth taken from the eleven Dutch regions plus one from Indonesia.

Some pictures of the white obelisk in the centre of Dam commemorating soldiers who fell in the last world war.

ROYAL PALACE

A fine example of classical Dutch architecture, it was designed by Jacob van Campen and built between 1648 and 1655. Constructed on 13,659 piles, needed to create a solid base in the marshy ground, it was originally built to take the place of the previous town hall, which had been completely destroyed by fire. Louis Bonaparte, the brother of Napoleon, made it his royal palace when he became King of Holland in 1808, though he abdicated only two years later. The severely simple appearance of the facade is what strikes the viewer first. It has four orders of windows, above which is a triangular pediment containing sculptures by Artus Quellijn the Younger, an artist from Antwerp. The statues represent the city of Amsterdam surrounded by Neptune and other mythical sea creatures, including nymphs and tritons, which pay homage to her wealth and power. The harmonious exterior of the palace is completed by an octogonal tower and cupola. Severely simple outside, the palace is splendidly decorated inside: for this decoration the artists commissioned included Ferdinand Bol, a pupil of Rembrandt, Govert Flinck and Sijmen Bosboom, while Rombout Verhulst was one of the most important sculptors.

The imposing façade of the Royal Palace.

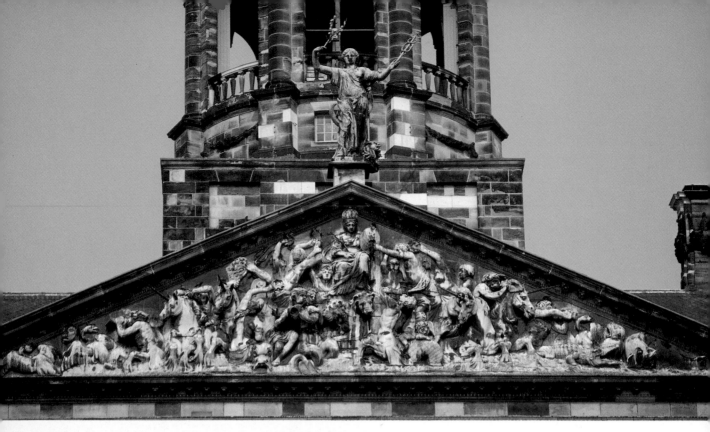

The pediment sculpted by Artus Quellijn crowning the main block of the Royal Palace.

One of the bas-reliefs that decorate the Court Room in the Royal Palace.

The Citizens room in the Royal Palace.

Nieuwe Kerk rebuilt in late Gothic style after the fire in 1452.

NIEUWE KERK

A huge fire in 1452, which left two thirds of the city of Amsterdam in ashes, also destroyed the original church standing on this site, next to where the Royal Palace was later built. The people of Amsterdam reconstructed the church, erecting a great late Gothic basilica with transept, choir, 14 chapels and two aisles, illuminated by 75 mullioned windows; above the nave is a wooden ceiling. The pride of the church is its *pulpit*, a Baroque masterpiece carved from wood by Albert Vinckenbrinck, who worked on it for no less than 13 years, completing it in 1649; it has the four Evangelists sculpted on the corners and the seven Works of Charity on its panels. In the choir are many tombs of famous Dutchmen, including that of Holland's greatest poet, Joost van den Vondel, and the grandiose marble tomb of Admiral de Ruyter, by Rombout Verhulst. From the time of King William I the Dutch sovereigns have been crowned in this church.

DAMRAK

The Damrak is a large thourough-fare that leads directly to the station. It is a commercial road, full of shops, antique shops, boutiques and pubs. Points of interest: the Museum of Sex at no. 26 and a well-stocked English bookshop, Allert de Lange, at no. 64.

A long red-brick building stands out to the left of the Damrak. It is a squat, imposing parallelepiped built between 1898 and 1903. It is one of Amsterdam's business centres: the Stock Exchange. It was built by Hendrik Petrus Barlage, pupil of Cuypers, and for its times it was listed among the ultramodern master-pieces of architecture.

Some aspects of teeming Dam, that gives rise to the Damrak thoroughfare.

A view of Damrak flanked by the Stock Exchange.

The Renaissance style Central Station building by Cuypers.

The 19th-century St. Nicholas's Church.

CENTRAL STATION

The Central Station of Amsterdam, built in 1889 on a small artificial island, is a typical example of the classical style of architecture known as Dutch Renaissance. Cuypers, the architect who had previously designed the Rijksmuseum, planned the station's exuberant facade and its two towers.

CHURCH OF ST NICHOLAS

In front of the Central Station buildings is St Nicholas, one of the many churches in Amsterdam. Built in 1875, it was consecrated to Roman Catholic worship in 1887. A picturesque festival in honour of the saint, whom the Dutch call Sinterklaas and who is the patron saint of children, young girls, merchants and fishermen, is held on the third Saturday of November.

Oudezijds Voorburgwal with the dome of St. Nicholas's Church in the background.

A partial view of Oude Kerk.

OUDEZIJDS VOORBURGWAL

This street, with the homonymous canal, is one of the most beautiful promenades in the Venice of the north; the waterway, dating back to the Middle Ages, reflects the façades of some of the most typical town houses and, in the background, the dome of St Nicholas.

OUDE KERK

The oldest church in Amsterdam, it was originally dedicated to St Nicholas, patron saint of sailors and of the city of Amsterdam itself. Recent excavations have shown that there was already a small church on the same site as the present Oude Kerk in the 13th century. The present Gothic church, now Protestant, was consecrated in 1306. Surrounded as it is by the low houses belonging to those who were

responsible for administering the church, the Oude Kerk towers over all the buildings clustered around it, and this adds emphasis to its already imposing mass. The bell-tower has a carillon of 47 bells, of which the renowned François Hemony cast 14 in 1658. On the top of it is a fine wooden steeple designed by Joost Janszoon Bilhamer and built in 1566; it is 220 ft high. The interior, which like the rest of the church has been damaged, rebuilt, altered and restored over the centuries, has a nave and two aisles; above the nave is a wooden barrel vault resting on 42 cylindrical pillars. Although the 38 altars which once added even more splendour to the Oude Kerk have since disappeared, the interior of the church still shows signs of its past glory. From the Renaissance period it still has three stained glass windows in the Chapel of Our Lady: they were designed in 1555 by Pieter Aertszoon and depict the *Death of the Virgin, the Adoration of the Shepherds* and the *Good Tidings*. Many famous Dutchmen are buried here, including the wife of Rembrandt, Saskia van Uylenburgh, the painter Carel van Mander, the organist Jan Pieterszoon and the explorer Kilaen van Rensselaer, who was one of the founders of Nieuwe Amsterdam, the city which was later to become known as New York.

AMSTELKRING MUSEUM

Ons' lieve heer op solder: literally translated it means to the Good Lord in the Granary. The only Catholic chapel still standing of the 60 clandestine churches of the Calvinist period, today it is a small museum, a typical Dutch house facing one of Amsterdam's most spectacular canals.

These were hard times for the town, tolerance being sacrificed for a Protestant unitary movement. The Reform triumphed and the Catholics were forced to hold their services in secret churches concealed behind innocent looking façades. The chapel at no. 40 was called the "Stag" after its founder's nickname. It was built between 1661 and 1663 by an enlightened trader, Jan Hardman. It consisted of two small houses on the canal, but in place of the attic, Hardman arranged and built a consecrated church, evidence of tolerance in a country which was going through the depths of repression.

Two stained-glass windows of the Chapel of Our Lady (the "Annunciation" and the "Death of the Virgin Mary").

The Chapel "To the Good Lord in the Granary..."

A view of Oudezijds Voorburgwal over which Oude Kerk looks.

Some typical homes of the Oudezijds Voorburgwal; the outstanding ones at 14, 19 and 187 all date back to the 17th century.

TYPICAL HOUSES OF THE OUDEZIJDS VOORBURGWAL

This canal is lined with handsome examples of typically Dutch dwellings, among which the one at No. 14, built in the first years of the 17th century, stands out. The house has what is known as a "step gable" and many windows with shutters all over the facade, as if the people who lived here wanted to enjoy the sunlight as much as possible, letting it flood into all the rooms. The rooms themselves were sober, the furnishings few, the floor uncovered: a simple place in all respects. In contrast, the design of the house at No. 19 in the same street, built in 1656 as the stone high on the facade says, shows the richest sense of imagination.

It has two huge dolphins, the largest in all Amsterdam, on either side of the so-called "neck gable" which crowns the house. The dolphins are linked by huge strings containing countless shells, yet another example of the life and emblems of the sea which recur in various forms throughout the architecture of Amsterdam. There is another example of a house with a neck gable at No. 187 Oudezijds Voorburgwal. This dwelling, built in 1663 and belonging originally to a merchant, is also called - understandably - the house with the "façade of pillars": the first four pillars are of the Tuscan order, the next four are Ionic and the top two are Corinthian, all out of brick. At the top are two nude statues of an Indian and a Negro, leaning against a pile of merchandise, including ropes and rolls of tobacco. A scroll in the centre hides the arm of the hoist used to lift goods up to the storeroom, the door of which is below: the storeroom and private residence of the merchant were thus one and the same building. The façade was richly adorned with festoons of fruit, scrolls and ovals which catch the light. The more sober and simple the lower part of the house was, the richer the decoration on the upper section.

Another evocative picture of the canal.

STADSBANK VAN LENING

These buildings, standing at the corner of the Oudezijds Voorburgwal and the Enge Lombardsteeg, were used until 1550 as storehouses for peat (as can be seen from the plaque on the entrance). In 1614 a municipal loan office was set up in them and in 1616 the buildings were converted by Hendrick de Keyser to house the bank known as the Stadsbank van Lening. The playwright Gerbrand Adriaenszoon Bredero (1585-1618) used the area around here, full of life and colour being the site of many small markets, as the setting for his lively comedies.

HOUSE OF THE THREE CANALS

At the point in which the Oudezijds Voorburgwal and the Oudezijds Achterburgwal meet, there is one of Amsterdam's most charming spots:

The Stadsbank van Lening on Oudezijds.

The House of the Three Canals.

two bridges in quick succession which cut the long, transversal canals of the town's historic centre and Grimburgwal. A magnificent house featuring an antique library is emblematic of this small paradise: the House of the Three Canals situated at their junction.

UNIVERSITY

To the left of the House of the Three Canals stands an arch. It is the entrance to the old age home for men, the Oudemanhuispoort, today the seat of Amsterdam University. But this arcade which leads to another canal, the Kloveniersburgwal, is also famous for its book market held daily. Old gentlemen stand behind stalls worn with the passing of time; the whole gallery that permits access to the courtyard of the University is their territory. Authentic curios and very old editions are to be found.

The charming inner courtyard adjacent to the booksellers' gallery was the courtyard of the old age home founded in 1601. Amsterdam University was built in 1632. On the 8th January of that same year, an historian Gerardus Johannes Vossius gave the inaugural speech of a university whose aims included opening a breach in triunphant Calvinism and defending freedom. Amsterdam University immediately attracted the most lucid minds of Dutch culture, from the mathematician Hortensius to the jurist Cabelliau and from the doctor Blasius to the theologian Van Leuwen.

In 1840 the University was transferred to this old age home and the *statue of Vossius,* first professor of Amsterdam University, was placed in the inner courtyard.

The monument to Professor Gerardus Johannes Vossius in the University courtyard.

The inner courtyard of the university built in 1632.

A characteristic corner of the Grimburgwal.

ROKIN

On Rokin, one of the city's main streets, the facades of its houses blackened by time, the Dutch people have recently erected a statue on horseback of the young Queen Wilhelmina, one of their best loved sovereigns. She came to the throne at an early age in 1890, and because of her influence the image of Holland spread throughout the world was that of a vigorous but orderly and tolerant country. When Holland was invaded by Hitler's armies, the Queen remained steadfast, never ceasing to urge her people to resist the invaders, even when she went into exile in London with her Government. In 1948, after reigning for more than half a century, Wilhelmina abidcated in favour of her daughter Juliana. At the end of the second world war, to honour the spirit of resistance and the will for freedom which, even in the darkest years, had always been kept alive in the Dutch people, Wilhelmina had the following words added to the city's coat-of-arms: "Heroic, resolute and generous city".

The equestrian monument to Queen Wilhelmina on Rokin.

A typical corner of Rokin.

Two views of spacious Rokin featuring tourist boats moored.

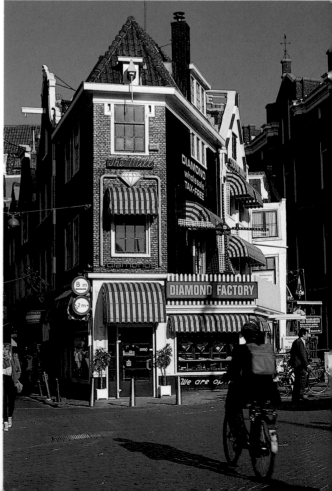

MUNTPLEIN

In Muntplein, which more than a real square is a large bridge between the Singel and Amstel, stands the Munttoren, the Mint Tower. It is a large baroque tower built in 1620 by the architect, Hendrick De Keyser right where the Regulierspoort, one of the oldest doors in Amsterdam, used to stand. When Louis XIV's armies invaded Holland in 1672, the Dutch government decided to transfer from French-occupied Utrecht to Amsterdam the state mint which was lodged in this very tower forming part of the city's vast defence system.

The Munttoren was damaged during one of Amsterdam's frequent fires. All that remained was a squat

Munttoren, or Mint Tower (1620), which looms up in Muntplein.

A mass of tulip bulbs on sale at the Flower Market.

stump in which they built a spire, that still rises up above the jerky traffic of Muntplein.

Today Mint Tower houses one of the most prestigious Delft ceramic shops, De Porcelyne Fles, the only one in Amsterdam offering every single piece of the vast original production of the Delft factory.

THE FLOWER MARKET

It is one of the pleasant sights of the city: a market that sells flowers, is open everyday (except Sundays) and occupies a whole bank of the Singel. It is a busy, bright bazaar which, alongside the inevitable tulips, sells everything, from exotic bananas to yucca and from coconuts to papyruses to end up with bonsai.

Some pictures of Bloemen Markt, the multicoloured flower market along the Singel.

Two views of the Singel.

THE SINGEL

It is Amsterdam's innermost canal, the narrowest circle of the half-moon of canals. Its name means ring or belt and it marked the boundary of the medieval town, the first Amsterdam which was built around the Dam and developed in the direction of Walletjes. Before the 17th century, the Singel was merely a ditch separating the town walls, which rose on the side of the odd numbers, from the gardens and lawns of Amsterdam's immediate outskirts. When the town passed the ditch, the walls no longer had any

reason for being there and houses sprung up along the banks of the Singel.

UNIVERSITY LIBRARY

Crowning this stark, classic building is the coat-of-arms of the city of Amsterdam. The crest is composed of the three crosses of St. Andrew on a shield with rampant lions supporting the crown of the Emperor Maximilian of Austria. Dutch literature encountered numerous problems with regard to circulation, mainly due to the difficulty of the language. Whereas the Dutch, who devote a great deal of time to the study of foreign languages, are

quite capable of reading texts in their original languages. Dutch works can only be read as far as the Flemish section of Belgium. In addition, Dutch books are not widely translated. The first auonomous features of Dutch literature came out around the 14th century when the dialect of the Netherlands began to make headway with respect to the then more widespread Flemish dialect. At the time that Holland emerged at the head of the anti-Spanish and anti-Austrian struggle, the language, once a national feeling arose, started to take hold. In fact, the first Dutch grammar boat, edited by Hendrik Spiegel, appeared around 1600, while only a few years later, Vondel laid the base for Dutch poetic language.

RONDE LUTHERSE KERK

The outstanding feature is without a shadow of doubt its copper dome 45-metres high. A fire destroyed it in 1822. It was then rebuilt, but its good fortune came to an end.
Today it is a centre for congress and conventions.

HOUSES OF THE GOLD
AND SILVER MIRRORS

In the shadow of the Lutheran Church is this interesting structure called the Houses of the "gouden en de Silveren Spiegel" (Gold and Silver Mirrors). They are twin houses, built with extraordinary symmetry and harmony in 1614.
The name derives partly from the fact that mirrors were built into the sandstone step gables of the houses and partly from the fact that the man who had the houses built was himself called Spiegel. Spiegel was a soapmaker and the father-in-law of Willem Backer, a mayor of the city, who later inherited the houses.
One of the town's most quaint houses was built at no. 7: the narrowest in absolute terms, no wider than a door. An authentic record and clever trick to avoid excessive taxes. In fact, in Amsterdam taxes on houses were paid according to the space that they occupied along the canals or streets; that is why all owners tried to build upwards instead of sidewards.

A partial view of Herengracht, known for the magnificent coping of its over 400 houses.

On the following pages: another picture of Herengracht, the city's residential canal.

Two views of the copper dome of what was the Lutheran church, now a conference centre: in the former, the "House of the Gold- and Silver-plated Mirrors" (1614) on the Singel.

The smallest house in town, at no. 7 on the Singel.

HERENGRACHT

The Herengracht, or Gentlemen's Canal, like the other canals called the Keizersgracht and the Prinsengracht, dates from 1612, when it was decided to dig a concentric series of canals surrounding the centre of the city. Reflected in the wide curves of the waters of the Herengracht are the aristocratic dwellings of the richest families in Amsterdam who once favoured this part of the city. The richest, most enlightened merchants came to live along this canal, competing with one another as to who had the most beautiful and largest house. It is the canal with the most impressive façades, sought-after coats-of-arms and imposing pediments. Over 400 houses on the Herengracht are considered national monuments. They are mainly occupied by offices and banks as their maintenance is too expensive for private ownership.

The characteristic depots turned into homes at nos. 37-39 and 43-45 along the canal.

The house at no. 274 crowned by an elaborate Rococo style balustrade.

The imposing Bartolotti House dating back to the early 17th century.

HOUSES ON THE HERENGRACHT

At Nos. 43-45 two recently restored warehouses are considered the oldest constructions on the canal.

At Nos. 170-172 is the building known as Bartolotti House. This double storey brick dwelling was built in 1615, possibly designed by Pieter de Keyser, for the brewer Willem van den Heuwel, who later became head of the Bartolotti banking house. The superb contrast between the red bricks and the white pilasters and decorations is beautifully mirrored in the waters of the canal. The house at No. 274, on the other hand, shows how quickly the artists of Amsterdam learnt to borrow styles from other countries. The magnificence of the Baroque style later transformed into the even greater elegance of Rococo, was soon imitated in many of the city's facades.

Between Nos. 338 and 270 one can admire some of the most beautiful houses of the Herengracht built between the mid-17th century and 1725. At no. 366 is the Bible Museum.

The most beautiful house on the canal is located at no. 475. It was built between 1668 and 1672 by a stone-rich merchant, Denys Nuyts and is a compact building with five windows per storey. In 1731 the window of a fabrics merchant, Petronella van Lennep de Neufville, made important changes to the house. She had the façade decorated by Daniel Marot, while the sculptor Ignatius van Logteren sculpted two female figures on the sides of the main window.

Last of all, there is the house at No. 605, belonging to Willet-Holthuysen, which was converted into a museum in 1895; it is a rare example of a building in a perfect state of preservation.

View of the Herengracht.

Other typical middle-class homes on Herengracht, including that of the trader Denys Nuyts at no. 475, in the bottom left hand corner, and the one at no. 605 housing the Willet-Holthuysen Museum in the bottom right hand corner.

Keizersgracht or Emperor's canal.

The well-known House of the Heads at 123 Keizersgracht.

KEIZERSGRACHT

The Emperor's Canal owes its name to Maximilian I, ruler of the Holy Roman Empire.
Keizersgracht connects the Amstel, in line with the famous wooden drawbridge - the Magere Brug - to Brouwersgracht. Its houses are not as imposing as those of parallel Herengracht, but they still keep their charm with some very valuable treasures. The most interesting strip of the canal lies between Westermarkt, Westerkerk square, and Vijzelstraat. During the last century, it was tradition after the Sunday church service to promenade in one's Sunday best along this part of the canal.

HOUSES ON KEIZERSGRACHT

The visitor who takes long walks through Amsterdam, letting his feet lead him where they will, is the one most likely to discover its superbly picturesque little corners, which appear suddenly and have an almost poetic simplicity. This, for example, is the point where Keizersgracht and Reguliersgracht meet, two canals whose waters come together here and are crossed by two old bridges. With the barge moving slowly along the canal, it has a quiet, otherworldly air. At No. 123 is the imposing residence built in 1622 for Pieter de Keyser in pure Dutch Renaissance style. From 1634 Louis de Geer lived in the house: he was a commercial magnate, involved in trade with Sweden, especially in the iron trade in which he established a virtual monopoly. The Czechoslovakian teacher Comenius also passed some time in the house, as a stone inscription on the facade says. The house is popularly known as the "Huis met de Hoofden", or House of the Heads, because of the Roman busts placed on the front of it. These are busts of classical gods,

though the story goes that they were the heads of burglars which had been cut off by a fearless maid belonging to the household. After the building at No. 446, one of the most imposing residences in the whole Keizersgracht, it is worth No. 615 with its typical neck visiting gable, decorated with figures reminiscent of the sea: nude men, tritons, and various denizens of the deep.

AMSTERDAM BY BIKE

It is no exaggeration to say that Holland is the land of bicycles: there are millions of them, and they are ridden by everyone.

Adults and children, men and women, from the humblest workers to members of the Royal family - everyone rides a bicycle, in good or bad weather, so that the bicycle has become not only the most common and commonsense form of transport but virtually the emblem or national symbol of Holland. To solve the long-standing problem of traffic on the canals, about ten years ago they introduced special bicycles, painted white to distinguish them and available to anyone who needed them for as long as required.

Two other elegant homes on Keizersgracht: no. 165 and no. 446.

Bicycles everywhere...

The gracious home at 739 Prinsengracht.

An old depot at 491 Prinsengracht.

PRINSENGRACHT

It is the most popular of Amsterdam's main canals and the outermost ring of its semicircumference. In fact, Princes Canal marks the outer boundary of the centre of Amsterdam. For a long strip, it skirts Jordaan, the city's most charming district.

WESTERKERK

After the Reformation had reached Holland, four Protestant churches were built in Amsterdam and named after the four cardinal points. The churches were, in the order of building: Zuiderkerk, Westerkerk, Noorderkerk and Oosterkerk (respectively, the south, west, north and east churches). This one, Westerkerk, is the largest Dutch Renaissance church in the whole of the Netherlands. It was begun by Hendrick de Keyser in 1619-1620, but he did not live to see it completed, and it was taken over and finished in 1638 by the architects Pieter de Keyser and Cornelis Dancker. The latter altered the design of the 285 ft tower, on top of which was placed a globe with a crown given by the Emperor Maximilian, who in 1489 had taken the city of Amsterdam under his protection. The superb interior, in the form of a double cross, was completed by Jacob van Campen in the purest neoclassical style. Adding to the already fine interior are the carillon, which has 47 bells cast by François Hemony, and a splendid *organ,* decorated in 1682 by Gerard de Lairesse, a pupil of Rembrandt. Inside the church is a *commemorative monument* to the great painter himself, even though it has never been known with absolute certainty whether Rembrandt is actually buried there.

Bell-tower and interior of
Westerkerk (1630-31) on
Prinsengracht.

The House of Anne Frank at 263 Prinsengracht.

Noorderkerk (1620) on Prinsengracht.

HOUSE OF ANNE FRANK

The House of Anne Frank is at No. 263 Prinsengracht. This young Jewish girl wrote the celebrated "Diary of Anne Frank" (called in Dutch "Het Achterhuis"), which was published in 1947. She hid in this house with her family and other Jews from 8 July 1942 to 4 August 1944, when their secret refuge was discovered and all the people in it arrested and deported. Anne Frank, taken to the concentration camp of Bergen-Belsen, died in March 1945, only two months before the liberation of Holland. Today the house contains thorough documentation on the deportation programme implemented by the Germans against the Dutch and is visited by a continual stream of people who will not, cannot or feel they ought not to forget the significance of Anne Frank's story.

NOORDERKERK

Noorderkerk, which has now been completely restored, was built in 1620 by Hendrick Jacobsz Staets.

The visitor is immediately struck by this church's appearance, different from so many other churches. In fact it was the first church to make a break with the ancient Roman Catholic architectural tradition, with its nave, transept, choir and altar. The Noorderkerk is in the form of a Greek cross, with four arms of equal length radiating out from the centre. The result is a solid, sober building, pure and essential in its forms, with no attempt at elegance except for its windows, including the mullioned windows which add a graceful touch to the facade.

PAPENEILAND

At the junction of Prinsengracht and Brouwersgracht is this pleasant corner of old Amsterdam, the Papeneiland, or Papists' Island. The name derives from a Carthusian monastery which once stood here, outside the city limits, on the site of what in now a small square between the narrow houses of this picturesque corner. The two bridges which meet here are called the Papiermolensluis (Paper Mill Sluice) and the Lekkere Sluis (Sweet Sluice); the latter name recalls the booths of pancake vendors which were once set up around here.

Papenailand, or Papists' Island, a delightful part of town.

The 17th century buildings that originally housed the Dutch East India and Dutch West India Companies.

HOMES OF THE INDIA COMPANIES

The merchants of Amsterdam in the 17th century, as soon as they had freed themselves from the domination of Spain, began to send hundreds of ships every year on long voyages around the world to establish trade with distant lands and to discover and explore new lands. The many trading companies which had grown up in Holland were combined in 1602 to form one big company, called the United East India Company or VOC (Vereenigde Oostindische Compagnie), in which the ambitious and powerful Amsterdammers invested. Alongside this company in 1621 another was formed with the name of the Geoctroyeerde Westindische Compagnei, or Chartered West India Company. Trading centres and colonies were thus created on the fertile coasts of the West Indies, and in 1625 the West India Company paid 60 florins to acquire the island of Manhattan at the mouth of the Hudson River. The colony founded here was called Nieuwe Nederland and its main city Nieuwe Amsterdam - later to become New York. The monumental appearance of the two buildings is a reminder still of the power and trading supremacy of these two companies and of the city which they represented in the 17th century. Standing out on the pediment of the East India Company facade is the famous coat-of-arms with the letters VOC (the company's initials) and the A of the city of Amsterdam. The other building, completed in 1642, is somewhat less monumental in appearance because of the colourful effect obtained by the skilful alternation of brick and sandstone.

CENTRAL POST OFFICE

KALVERSTRAAT

The Main Post Office, built in 1908 in Dutch Renaissance style.

Standing in front of the Royal Palace, the Central Post Office belongs in style to the Dutch Renaissance: with its exuberant decoration, it contributes to the harmonious effect of the other buildings around the square.

As the name itself (Calves' Street) and the carved stones on the house fronts suggest, this street was originally, in the Middle Ages, a cattle market. Later, in the 17th and 18th centuries, many booksellers and coffee merchants established themselves here. Today the street, running from the Dam to Muntplein, is one of the busiest and most pleasant in the city. It is lined with elegant shops and is always full of people, for not only tourists but also the Amsterdammers themselves love to stroll along it.

Four pictures of busy Kalverstraat, the shopping street of Medieval origin.

The stone arch leading from Kalverstraat to the Burgerweeshuis, what was originally Amsterdam's orphanage and is now the city's History Museum.

The Boys' Courtyard in the Burgerweeshuis.

The statue of Goliath, an automaton in full view in the restaurant situated in the old granary of the Burgerweeshuis.

BURGERWEESHUIS

At number 92 Kalverstraat a stone arch leads to the courtyards of the old orphanage or Burgerweeshuis of Amsterdam, today occupied by the Amsterdam History Museum. The building was built as a monastery dedicated to Saint Lucy and remained as such for over one hundred years, from 1414 to 1578. It was only then that the building underwent its first radical transformation, lodging the city's orphans. This situation lasted for over four centuries: in 1960 the orphanage closed its doors to open them fifteen years later, on the seven hundredth anniversary of Amsterdam, as the prestigious premises of the City's History Museum. Through the arch on Kalverstraat (on which are engraved verses by the poet Vondel) one gains access to the boys' courtyard. To the left you will see cup-

boards where the orphans put their overalls and tools back after a day's work while to the right, the old granary of the convent now houses a restaurant, In de Oude Goliath. Its interior is dominated by the gigantic *statue of Goliath* flanked by the tiny *David*. From 1650 to 1682, Goliath was the main attraction of Amsterdam's amusememt park: thanks to a simple device, his eyes roll and his head moves. From the girls' courtyard which follows on the boys' courtyard, one gains access to the Museum. The Amsterdam History Museum narrates the tales of the city from prehistoric times to the present day. The rapid growth of Amsterdam, its port, the fortunes of the Golden Century and minor events of daily life are narrated across 17 halls that do not fail to describe the continuous struggle of the inhabitants of Amsterdam against the sea.

The Girl's Courtyard in the Burgerweeshuis.

The entrance gate to the Burgerweeshuis on St. Luciensteeg.

A view of the Begijnhof, the green oasis of peace which offers refuge from the din of Kalverstraat.

BEGIJNHOF

It is a place of absolute peace and quiet, an idyllic oasis and an unexpected refuge from the uproar of Kalverstraat.

The entrance leads to a sort of vast courtyard in the centre of which is a lovely lawn surrounded by numerous small houses kept in perfect order. Old ladies who go for strolls and drink tea in their gardens, flowers everywhere, an incredible sense of calm and two chapels facing one another together form the Begijnhof.

It was founded in 1346 by a group of women, Beguines, who aspired to living in a religious community without restricting themselves to the

rigid rules of a cloistered life. They did not take the vow and behaved as lay sisters: they all kept their own little houses, personal liberty and freedom but they dedicated their lives to the poor and ill.

In 1578 the Protestant Reform deprived the Beguines of their chapel which was then assigned to the Presbyterians. It is the church still standing in the centre of the Beijnhof. Protestantism did not bend the community who remained Catholic and continued to hold their religious services, changing house each time in order not to be discovered. The Catholic chapel in front of the English Church is just an old house transformed into a place of worship.

Every year on the 2nd May, visitors to the Begijnhof can observe flowers placed on a dark stone, to the side of the English Church. It is the simple *tomb of Cornelia Arents.* On her death, this Beguine asked for a simple burial to expiate the guilt of her family who had been converted to Protestantism. Her wish was not granted and Cornelia was initially placed inside the church. Only that in the morning the coffin containing Cornelia's body was found outside the chapel door. This phenomenon recurred three times until this Beguine's dying wishes were fulfilled.

Today Beguines no longer live here. The last of them died in 1971 and the Begijnhof lodges poor old ladies on their own who pay a nominal rent.

At number 34 Begijnhof is situated the oldest house in Amsterdam, the only one still in wood after an order of the city government prevented the construction of new houses in inflammable materials. The house at number 34 dates back to the 15th century and the cul-de-sac which passes in front of it shows some of the most beautiful coats-of-arms of the city.

15th and 16th century homes overlooking the Begijnhof courtyard.

The oldest house of the Begijnhof and in the city. It stands at no. 34 and dates back to the 15th century. It is the only wooden construction to be found in Amsterdam, after the authorities prohibited the construction of buildings with such highly inflammable material in 1521.

The representative monument to the Beguine.

SPUI

On the wide Spui, one of the most interesting streets, stands the Maagdenhuis, the House of the Virgins. It used to be a Catholic orphanage built in 1787. Today it belongs to Amsterdam University. On turning to the right, proceed in the direction of one of the intellectual centres of the Dutch capital. In the centre stands a tiny, mocking statue, *Het Lieverdje*, the Amsterdam's impertinent "urchin", one of the city's ironic symbols. Close to the statue of the rogue is one of the most popular pubs, the Hoppe, a very crowded meeting place for both students and artists, often written up by writers and journalists.

Amsterdam's "urchin" ("Het Lieverdje").

Characteristic bars on Spui.

LEIDSESTRAAT

Leidsestraat is one of the busiest streets in town as it is one of Amsterdam's business centres with its shops, cafés and countless company headquarters and international airline companies. It features numerous constructions of various architectural levels: important charming buildings blend in with more ordinary ones.

Two pictures of pulsating Leidsestraat that leads from Spui.

Two buildings on the street, sometimes enriched by fascinating decorations.

LEIDSEPLEIN

Not so very long ago, it was prohibited to travel into the city of Amsterdam in carts or wagons, so the merchants and travellers who had to enter the centre of the city were forced to leave their vehicles in huge squares on the outskirts of the city. At the beginning of the road which led to Leiden was Leidseplein, surrounded, like all the other similar squares, by buildings used as warehouses, ''parking areas'' for carts and wagons, and blacksmiths' and carpenter' workshops. Not forgetting, naturally, the inns and alehouses, places for eating and relaxing.

Four moments of the busy life in Leidseplein, the wildest square in Europe, an improvised stage for many young performers.

The Civic Theatre on Leidseplein.

The American Hotel, built on Leidseplein in 1897 in Art Nouveau style.

It is a window that looks onto the world: you could see it passing in front of you without ever having to move at all. All you have to do is wait. Cafés, theatres, beer-houses, clubs, all types of meeting-places, legendary pubs, taverns, street shows, mines, clowns, afro musicians and hard rockers contribute to making Leidseplein the most unrestrained square in Europe.
In Leidseplein you will find everything imaginable: the Paradiso, the deconsecrated church occupied by Provos during the sixties and since then a sanctuary for rock music, and on the other side of the square Melkweg all lit up as well as a large abandoned cheese factory transformed into the home of improvised play-acting and a stage-setting for every young Dutch actor.

CIVIC THEATRE AND AMERICAN HOTEL

In the centre of Leidseplein you will find the Civic Theatre and the Uit Bureau, the information and booking office that covers every show in town. Do not fail to visit the fantastic American Hotel nextdoor. It was built by W. Kromhout in 1897 in pure Art Nouveau style. It is a surprising mixture of the architect's kitsch and a work of art. Everyting is perfect down to the most minor details: from the candlesticks to the windows and from the furnishings to the mosaics. Even the waiters are impeccable while clients make a din. Take a look at the serious minded gentlemen sipping their tea at the newspapers' table; they are mainly journalists and writers who come to reread their work in one of Amsteram's most historic places. It was here that Mata Hari, spy and high class lady, wished to celebrate her wedding.

SINGELGRACHT

Singelgracht is the outermost of the old canals in Amsterdam. This wide, windy canal was heavily urbanized as from the second half of the 17th century. The numerous activities carried out there and the social class of its inhabitants are still reflected in the appearance of the buildings flanking the canal. In fact, these buildings often differ from Amsterdam's regular houses - tall and high - and are reminiscent of Central European taste.

Two partial views of Singelgracht, flanked by elegant Central European-style homes.

VONDELPARK

It is named after the great Dutch poet Joost van den Vondel, who was born in 1587 and died in 1679. It is a magnificent park covering over one and a half kilometres and almost 50 hectares wide. Lawns, small lakes, plays of water, a rose-garden and a tea-room create a dreamy atmosphere right in the heart of the city. It is Amsterdam's Bois de Boulogne: on Sundays it is thronged by thousands of city-dwellers in overalls, racing on bicycles or roller-skates, taking the dog for a walk or simply stretching out on the grass. Right throughout the sixties, during the summer, Vondelpark was the noctural destination of vagrant hippies. Their little Saturday market aroused the curiosity of crowds. Nowadays, during the summer months, open air concerts, children's plays and marches of talented music bands are held in Vondelpark.

Two views of Vondelpark; at the top, the monument to the poet Joost van den Vondel.

Two façades of the Rijksmuseum designed in Neo-Gothic style by Pieter Cuypers and opened in 1885.

THE RIJKSMUSEUM

In 1808 the King of Holland, Louis Bonaparte, placed on the throne by his brother, the Emperor Napoleon, decided to make Amsterdam not only the political but also the cultural capital of his kingdom. This was when the Town Hall on the Dam became the Royal Palace, and the king also created a royal art museum with its collections housed in several rooms on the palace's first floor.

When Napoleon had the Kingdom of Holland incorporated into that of France, this became the Dutch Museum, which because of the pressure of events remained here rather than being transferred elsewhere as planned. Then the new king, William I of the House of Orange, came to the throne, and he directed that the collections (which in the meantime had grown both in quantity and in quality) should remain in Amsterdam and that the museum should be called the Rijksmuseum van Schilderijen, or Museum of the Kingdom of the Netherlands. The works were later transferred to the Trippenhuis, an aristocratic dwelling built between 1660 and 1664 by the rich Trip brothers, where the museum was opened to the public in February 1817. It remained here for about seventy years, although its space problems became more and more serious as the number of works it possessed continued to grow. In 1862 a competition was announced for the design of a new museum building, and 21 architects took part.

Only ten years later the design submitted by P.J.H. Cuypers was accepted, and on 13 July 1885 the Rijksmuseum of Amsterdam, a grandiose building made from red brick in the neo-Gothic style, was officially opened. It has more than 260 rooms, containing not only masterpieces of painting but also superb prints, furniture, ceramics and other works of art.

Rembrandt van Rijn:
The Company of Cloth-Manufacturers

This impressive canvas dated and signed in the top righthand corner (Rembrandt s. 1662) was commissioned by the Cloth-Manufacturers' Guild with its headquarters in Staalhof; here it remained until 1771 when it was transferred to the Amsterdam town-hall. In Rembrandt's artistic career, this is the last of his great group portraits. These were already the most difficult years for the great Dutch artist: the sale of his home and collections - from which, amongst other things, he received very little - the dwindling of assignments, and as a result, very little work. Yet his painting is pervaded by a great serenity. The five characters, plus a servant in the background, are portrayed around a table and look as though they have been interrupted in the middle of doing something. Their expressions are severe, yet serene; their faces are calm and attentive. The light breaks up and bathes the whole composition, lights up the drape on the table, touches upon a corner of the wall, and plays with the wide, white collars of the gentlemen. This is one of the finest examples of that perfect harmony that Rembrandt knew how to achieve in his famous large-scale paintings.

Rembrandt van Rijn:
Self-portrait

Rembrandt left about seventy self-portraits. In fact, the artist loved doing portraits of himself with a sort of brutal sincerity and attention to detail. Therefore, in the absolute absence of beauty, the human aspect comes to the fore. Rembrandt does not pose nor disguise himself.
He looks at himself in the mirror, penetrates his innermost thoughts and, above all, he allows himself to be observed. The result is a real, sincere portrait with great psychological introspection.

Rembrandt van Rijn:
Night Watch

This painting by Rembrandt, one of his masterpieces and indeed a masterpiece of Western culture, was completed by the painter when he was 36 in 1642. The large canvas (measuring 4.38 by 3.59 metres or about 14 ft by 10ft) was commissioned to celebrate the visit of Marie de Medici to the city. Rembrandt painted the company of Captain Frans Cocq and his lieutenant Willem van Ruytenburch, a volunteer militia group before the march. The name by which the painting is now universally known was given to it in the 18th century when, because of oxidation of the paint, the canvas came to acquire a "nocturnal" appearance. Rembrandt, fascinated by all the artistic problems in the Baroque period, ranging from that of movement to the expression of individual emotion, broke decisively with the then fashionable tradition of group portraits and placed the figures in his painting in dramatic poses, as if they were actors standing before an open curtain. Making skilful use of line and colour and wielding the brush with consummate genius, he gives us a sense of movement which seems to be communicated from one figure to the next. At the same time each figure in the work is given his own psychological identity. Each gesture is carefully weighed and measured, so that it is never excessive. Other details add relish such as the figures of the children and the dog barking. Rembrandt creates un unforgettable impression of a group of people moving slowly out of the shadows into the light and towards the spectator.

Jan Vermeer van Delft:
Woman reading a letter

The generation after Rembrandt's produced an artist who, despite his copious production, showed how great art did not depend entirely on the importance of the subject. Jan Vermeer van Delft knew how to create a universe formed by intimacy and the small things in life: interiors of middle-class homes, everyday people, daily occupations and simple gestures. His great painting belongs to that Dutch upper middle-class who had already conquered the seas and had gathered together a solid, yet contained wealth, which was never flaunted. In the Woman reading a letter, painted between 1662 and 1663 and reputed to be a portrait of his wife, Catherine -who was pregnant at the time -, our attention is immediately captured by the composed profile of the woman holding a piece of paper, dressed in a soft pale-blue jacket that reveals and outlines the rounded shapes of maternity. From a window to the left, which we cannot see but know is there, a ray of light comes in, hits the table and spreads over the figure of the woman.

Jan Vermeer van Delft:
The Milk-Maid

Inside an anonymous kitchen, a woman with an absolutely common appearance is intent on pouring milk from a jug; it is one of the countless banal occupations that Vermeer loved to depict. From the grey wall that serves as a backdrop emerges the energetic silhouette of the housewife, with her course brightly-coloured clothing. The slow gesture of pouring the milk into the large bowl blends in perfectly with the still life represented by the bread in the basket. Here too light plays a fundamental role, outlining the room, breaking up in the woman's bonnet and, for a split second, it gives life to and transforms what was just lifeless space before.

The Van Gogh Museum opened in 1973.

Two rooms in the Van Gogh Museum.

VAN GOGH MUSEUM

It is a square building in glass and raw cement with large halls and bright, wide open spaces. This modern building was built by Gerry Rietveld to house Van Gogh's paintings. It was opened in 1973 and contains the largest, most important collection of Van Gogh's works donated by his brother Theo and his son Vincent. This museum must be visited at all costs. The Van Gogh

Museum contains 200 of his paintings, 500 of his drawings and 700 letters written by him. Works of contemporaries such as Gauguin and Toulouse-Lautrec are also on display.

The Museum is structured on four floors in the form of galleries. Van Gogh's works are divided up into the periods of his life in artistic succession. On the ground floor are souvenirs of the artist including his private letters.

At the end of the last century, a short article appeared in a provincial newspaper: "Sunday 27th July, a 37 year old, Dutch artist by the name of Van Gogh passing through

Auvers-sur-Oise shot himself in the countryside. He was only injured; he dragged himself to his room where he died two days later". This describes the death of one of the greatest contemporary artists, Vincent Van Gogh, known to be a desperate madman. This was in 1890. Van Gogh was born on the 30th March 1853 in Grootzundert in Brabant of a family of Protestant clergymen. For a short while he followed in his father's footsteps studying theology and became assistant-clergyman. But it was not a vocation for him. He discovered art and painting and during the last ten years of his life, he dedicated all

his time to painting. He did over 800 paintings, to which over 800 drawings must be added. He corresponded frequently with his brother Theo. In the last years of his life spent in the Camargue, at Arles and Auvers, Van Gogh produced his most famous masterpieces: paintings that represented a public confession of dramas, distress and the great strength and passion of one of the most lucid men of his time.

Self-portrait

This canvas, painted in Paris in the late summer of 1887, shows how much Van Gogh learnt from Seurat's lesson on Pointillisme, but at the same time how he gave it his own interpretation, distorting it. The technique of Divisionism, or making a series of blobs of primary colours, was turned into nervous brush-strokes, expressing the artist's frame of mind. Van Gogh wrote, "... sometimes emotions are so strong that one works without realizing that one is working..."; hallucinated and vibrant, this self-portrait is evident proof of what he said. "It is not easy to paint one-self", he once said, yet we know of at least thirty-five self-portraits he did using a mirror.

Potato eaters

There are about a dozen preliminary drawings and three paintings on this subject; this particular one was painted between April and May 1885 in Nuenen, where Van Gogh's father had been appointed clergy-man and where the artist remained for two years, drawing and painting houses, people and landscapes. Van Gogh was deeply saddened by the hardship and labours of local peasants and miners, and that is what he wanted to convey in his paintings. In a letter to Theo, he wrote, "... it is quite clearly a paint-ing of peasants. If a painting of peasants smacks of lard, smoke and potato steam, all the better..." That is why his range of colour was reduced to browns and drawings became strong, ungraceful lines to describe heavy, clumsy figures. As he goes on to say in a letter to his brother, those bony hands, deformed by hard labour in the fields and which pick potatoes from the common plate, are the very hands that dug up the earth in which the potatoes grew. Van Gogh is not interested in whether the painting appeals or not; he is only interested in what he sees and feels. And if anyone "prefers to interpret peasants in a sickly sweet way, let him get on with it".

Vase with sunflowers

In Arles, Van Gogh was anxiously awaiting his friend Paul Gauguin. He rented a small house with a yellow façade; the interior was only decorated with a series of twelve paintings depicting yellow sunflowers. Yellow is the colour that distinguishes Van Gogh's activity in Arles; this one painted in January 1889 is one of the most beautiful of this famous series of paintings. The composition is a rhapsody in yellow and the brush-stroke is continuous and emotional almost to the point of being aggressive; he does not just create the volume of flowers, but defines their very outlines. He wrote to his brother, "I have reached the stage in which I no longer draw the picture in charcoal... if one wants a good drawing, one must do it directly in colour". In fact, Van Gogh went as far as squeezing the tube of colour onto the canvas; then, with large brush-strokes, he broke up the colour and created stunning masses of sunflowers, obtaining a mosaic effect that the artist himself compares to the stained-glass windows of a church.

Field of wheat with a flight of crows

The Breton village of Auvers-sur-Oise, with its "rugged beauty and picturesque countryside" was the last port of call in Vincent Van Gogh's tormented life. Five months had passed since the last attack in Saint-Rémy and the change in air in Auvers seemed to have had a benificial effect on him. In a letter of July 1890, he wrote to his mother: "I am completely absorbed in this endless plain of wheat fields against a backdrop of hills, as huge as the sea... I am calm, almost too calm, that is to say, I am in the frame of mind to paint these things".

But this painting, completed before 9th July, features nothing of the calm so badly desired by Van Gogh. It seems as though it was painted during a fit of destructive violence; the colour is applied by furious strokes of a spatula and not a brush. Gone are the days of the quiet, almost sleepy Breton countryside, but that does not matter to Van Gogh; this is what he feels and sees; nature is deformed because that is all his painting could express. No gnarled olive trunks or contorted cypress shapes and no human presence to populate and enliven this deserted sea of wheat; only a dramatic flight of crows in a stormy sky. In this painting Van Gogh did not have to strive "... to express sadness and extreme solitude", as he wrote to Theo in July. The latter two were by this stage his only companions, because Van Gogh thought it pointless to write about anything else. It was to these fields

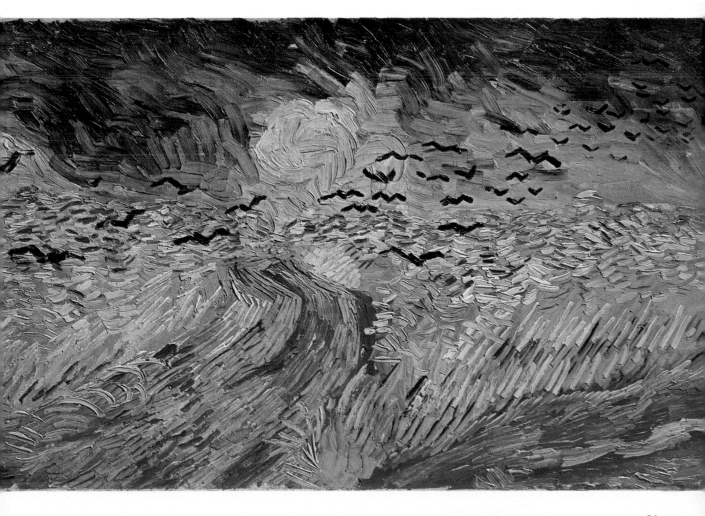

that the artist went on 27th July with just the gun he used to shoot himself and an unfinished letter to Theo.

"Well, as for my work, I am risking my life and have half lost my mind": never in Van Gogh's life had his sentiments and creations been so well identified.

The Langlois Bridge

It was one of van Gogh's favourite subjects; he started painting it immediately after his arrival in Provence in February 1888. Apart from numerous watercolours and drawings, four versions of this subject exist. Van Gogh is attracted by the play on light, transparency, the reflections in water and the satured atmosphere; the whole painting is penetrated by indescribable serenity. When van Gogh settled in Arles, he was immediately struck by its evocative landscape bathed in Southern light and by that "extraordinarily beautiful Nature" that his painting technique also changed. In fact, as he wrote to his sister "... Nature in the South cannot be depicted with the palette of the North. Today my palette is full of colours..."

Still Life

Painted at the end of 1888, this pair of clogs ideally formed part of the series of paintings that van Gogh dedicated over the years to daily life. His painting is full of empty chairs, deserted rooms and abandoned objects. In their extreme realism, they lose their everyday banality to symbolize man's solitude.

The Neo-Renaissance building that houses the Stedelijk Museum.

STEDELIJK MUSEUM

It is the municipal museum of the city of Amsterdam and contains one of the most important collections of modern art in Europe. Its collections mainly concern the 19th and 20th Centuries in Holland and France with their best painters: Cézanne, Monet, Picasso, Matisse, Mondriaan, Malevitch, Chagall and Dubuffet.

The red-brick building on elegant Paulus Potterstraat which houses the Stedelijk Museum was built between 1893 and 1895 by the architect. A.W. Weissmann. It is another example of the Dutch Renaissance and its façade is distinguished by numerous niches occupied by statues of Amsterdam's leading artists which inevitably include Hendrick de Keyser and Jacob van Campen. The Stedelijk Museum was built thanks to the generosity of Amsterdam's leading collectionists: the Town Council decided to build the museum when Amsterdam received the collection of Sophia Augusta de Bruyn as a donation in 1891.

Initially the Stedelijk Museum accepted all kinds of collections: the History of Archery, the Museum for measuring time, Oriental art and the museums of the history of medicine. It was only in 1952, when these collections were transferred to more suitable places, that the Stedelijk Museum concentrated only on modern art.

The wing of the museum on van Baerlestraat, flanked by bronze sculptures by contemporary artists, and the rear of the building.

The façade of the Concertgebouw opened in 1888 on van Baerlestraat.

CONCERTGEBOUW

The Concertgebouw was built thanks to the pride of six Dutch businessmen needled by the ferocious irony of a magazine that accused the inhabitants of Amsterdam of having no knowledge of art because art does not make money. It was laid on thick by Johannes Brahms who, invited to Amsterdam in 1879, did not hesitate to define the Dutch as appalling musicians. This was too much. The six men launched the challenge and in 1883

they supervised the bedding of the first pillars (2,186 in the end) on which the Concertgebouw was to be positioned.

Five years later the building was completed and on the 3rd November the new National Orchestra gave its first concert under the directorship of Willem Kes. Even though Kes remained director of the Concertgebouw for only seven years, he managed to implant a deep love for music in the Dutch people.

His successor, Willem Mengelberg, remained in office for half a century and introduced Mahler and Strauss, succeeding in organising

the stirring Mahler Festival.

Very soon the Concertgebouw became one of the most sought-after destinations of orchestras and composers even if it austere halls also opened their doors to classical music. Great artists such as Louis Armstrong, Count Basie, Lionel Hampton and Frank Sinatra invaded the Concertgebouw where the historic rock concerts of Frank Zappa and the Who were also held. On the other hand, just after it was opened, the Concert Hall was also rented by the Socialist International and organisers of an artistic cycling championship in 1896.

GELDERSEKADE

Although the appearance Amsterdam must have had in the Middle Ages has now almost completely disappeared, the city limits, which were intact until 1590, can still be distinguished. One of them is the canal called the Geldersekade, "kade" meaning wharf or quay. At the end of it is a fortified tower, the Shreierstoren (Weepers' Tower), which once marked the place where sailors embarked for voyages both to known lands and to countries still to be discovered. From here, on 4 April 1609, Henry Hudson set sail on the ship Half Moon, to land ultimately on the island of Manhattan, site of New York.

The Schreierstoren (1482) at the Prins Hendrikkade and Geldersekade crossing.

Houses overlooking Geldersekade, embellished by a whole series of coping.

The Waag, or Public Weighing-House during the Middle Ages, and St. Anthony's gate inserted in the 15th century circle of walls.

WAAG
(Sint Anthoniespoort)

Sint Anthoniespoort, or St Anthony's Gate, is one of the many traces which still remain in Amsterdam of its medieval origins. It is the only city gate left from that period, and was the city's eastern exit when Amsterdam was still surrounded by water. An inscription says that the first stone of the gate was laid on 28 April 1488. When the canal was drained in 1614 to allow a market-place to be built (the Oostermarkt, which was later to become the square occupied by the Nieuw-markt), the gate was left isolated as it appears today. In 1617 it was transformed into the Waaghuis, the Public Weighing House, with its five picturesque towers. A number of professional guilds came to occupy the upper floor, including those of the painters, the surgeons, the blacksmiths and the masons, while the ground floor continued to be used as a weighing house until 1819. Each guild had its own private entrance, separated from the others and decorated with emblems which distinguished it from them. The fine rooms of the masons' guild can still be admired, with the entrance sculpted by Hendrick de Keyser, as well as the circular theatre of the surgeons' guild in which Rembrandt painted his celebrated ''Anatomy Lesson''.

KLOVENIERS-
BURGWAL

Kloveniersburgwal, one of the canals that flanks the city's Medieval centre, breaks away from Nieuwmarkt Square to flow into the Amstel. At no. 12 Kloveniersburgwal, take a look at Jacob Hooy's pharmacy-herbalists's shop. One of Amsterdam's historic shops dating back to 1743, over 400 herbs are on sale here in a pleasant almost Liberty atmosphere, both for medical and cooking purposes.

Jacob Hooy's intriguing herbalist's shop dating back to the mid-18th century.

A view of Kloveniersburgwal with the Waag in the background.

The 17th century Trip House, one of the best-known, most luxurious houses in Amsterdam.

TRIPPENHUIS

The house of the Trips is a real Neoclassic palace. It was built by one of the greatest 17th century architects, Justus Vingboons, for the Trip brothers, Louis and Hendrik, stone-rich cannon manufactures and owners of iron mines in Sweden.
They were the grandsons of Louis de Geer, Holland's iron king in the 17th century. They wanted a house in keeping with their enormous wealth and managed to have one built between 1660 and 1664. They were not ungrateful to the family business that enabled such luxury: the *chimneys* of the Trippenhuis are in the shape of huge mortars. They were also generous: when it escaped a waiter's lips that he would have been happy with a house as large as the mere front door of the Trippenhuis, one of the Trip brothers did not hesitate to satisfy his request. In fact, facing the Trippenhuis on the other side of the canal at no. 26 stands an identical miniature house: the little Trippenhuis, dwelling-place of one of the Trips', lucky servants. Even after the end of the industrial empire, the Trips' house remained one of the most important houses in Amsterdam; it even housed the Rijksmuseum when William I decided to transfer it from the halls of the Royal Palace, after the abdication of Louis Bonaparte.
The museum remained there until it was plain that the collections could no longer fit into the house; the Rijksmuseum was installed in the Trippenhuis in 1816 and remained there until Queen Wilhelmina inaugurated the final premises of the museum.

OLD JEWISH DISTRICT

From the 16th century onwards, the Dutch capital was the only possible refuge for thousands of Jews persecuted right throughout Europe. For them Amsterdam represented the "Mokum", the only safe city in which to live. The first Jews to take refuge there escaped the Catholic inquisition. They came from Spain and wanted to call themselves Sephardi, from the Jewish name for the Iberian Peninsula. Subsequently, after the fall of Antwerp (1585), the Jewish traders from those towns, who managed to survive, arrived; they were the first diamond

Modern buildings on Raamgracht and Zuiderkerk Square.

cutters to live in Amsterdam. Recently, this district underwent radical restructuring to build the underground. The modernizing of all the buildings, in striking contrast with the rest of the centre, has created an "historic" clash between this very recent architecture and the canal on which they are reflected, one of the oldest.

ZUIDERKERK

Built in 1603 by the omnipresent Hendrick de Keyser, the Zuiderkerk or South Church is a Protestant church dominated by a high belltower; during the summer months, it is possible to climb up it. The Zuiderkerk is reliving today a new golden era after decades of abandon; in 1929, in fact the last religious services were held there. The parish was becoming depopulated and the ecclesiastic authorities decided to suppress services in the Zuiderkerk. Nowadays, after many years of restoration, the Zuiderkerk is used for cultural festivals.
Access is gained to the Zuiderkerk through a small arch crowned by a skull. It is to be found between Nos. 130 and 132 of Sint Antoniesbreestraat.
In Zuiderkerk Square the old clashes with the new because the exterior of the old apse of the Zuiderkerk is surrounded by modern, elegant buildings. It is also worth mentioning the slope of the square, probably inspired by that of the Piazza del Campo in Siena.

The Zuiderkerk bell-tower built in tha early 17th century by Hendrick de Keyser.

On the following page, a view of Oudeschans and the old storehouses along the canal.

OUDESCHANS

The Oudeschans is one of the widest canals in which the Amstel was deviated. In 1883, the canal had its moment of glory when an English youth organised a series of fantastic apparitions. He disturbed Amsterdam's quiet, the residents along the canal were sure they had seen a ghost dance. Nearby is one of the most photographed corners in Amsterdam: Sint Antoniesluis. This closed bridge offers an excellent view and a chance to take in the city's special atmosphere.

MONTELBAANSTOREN

It is a red-brick tower typical of those seen in Amsterdam. It was built in 1512 purely for defence reasons. It was to protect the Latage, the basin for repairing and storing big Dutch ships. It was merely a lowered tower; in 1606, Hendrick de Keyser added its spire. Today this tower houses the offices in charge of the closing of canals and water flow in Amsterdam.

The Montelbaanstoren (1512).

Sint Anthoniesluis, a sluice bridge on Oudeschans.

HOUSE OF REMBRANDT

In this house in Sint Anthonies breestraat (corresponding today to Nos. 4-6 Jodenbreestraat) the great Rembrandt lived from 1639 to 1658. It might be said that he lived his last happy years here, when he was with his wife Saskia: she died in 1642, only six months after the birth of their son Titus, the same year in which Rembrandt completed what is generally considered his greatest masterpiece, "The Night Watch". Here too Rembrandt began his art collection which, more than anything else, was intended to pay off the debts which weighed him down. But the fine collection was no help, since the painter was forced to abandon his house because of insolvency. Converted into a museum in 1911, the house unfortunately suffered the damage and destruction which in the second world war hit Amsterdam's densely populated Jewish quarter, the heart of which was here. Only some of the houses survived including the house of Rembrandt, which thus serves to commemorate the time when the painter lived and worked here.

WATERLOOPLEIN

Only one hundred years ago, this square was regularly flooded by the Amstel; as a result no markets were held there. In 1883, it was made safe, shortly giving rise to a picturesque flea market selling books, clothes and any kind of objects and fancy goods. The old square was recently revamped; according to plans by the architect Holzbauer and with government approval, 3000 pylons are to be sunk into the ground to build the New Opera Theatre and New Town Hall. The latter had been badly needed for some time, as the old building on the Dam had been inadequate since 1808 and, by

Rembrandt's house on Sint Anthoniesbreestraat.

94

this stage, the Prinsenhof space was no longer large enough. The New Opera Theatre is the result of a stroke of genious on the part of the above-mentioned architect Holzbauer who suggested combining the two buildings in the same square, placing both of them in an easily accessible area and putting an end to the dispute as to the best area. The modern, round-lined building, surrounded by glass on the outside, is reflected in the waters of the Nieuwe Herengracht and is one of the most prestigious theatres in town.

Buildings that sprung up recently on Waterlooplein: the New Opera House and Town Hall.

FLEA MARKET

Each city has its own colourful second-hand market: Amsterdam lays out its wares albeit antique or just old, simple or pretentious, rare or common, but interesting or amusing in any case.

In Amsterdam's most famous market, you can find literally everything amongst unprecedented confusion and continuous bartering. They will try to sell you an old gramophone with no hope of working, broken records, worn-out books, second hand clothes and trinkets. But, with a bit of patience and luck, you might manage to find something you have been searching for in vain for years. But do not expect to find great bargains: the vendors are fully aware of the value of their goods. Right throughout the morning, Amsterdam's flea market is full of people who protest, contract, buy and ruin themselves in order to buy chips of a glorious past or search for missing cooking utensils which cost too much in the shops. The flea market is one of the places in which to idle away one's time.

Four colourful pictures of the Flea Market.

VISSERPLEIN

Various important buildings overlook this vast square: first and foremost, the Church of Moses and Aaron, which faces sideways onto the square, and, to the sides, the major synagogues in Amsterdam.

CHURCH OF MOSES AND AÄRON

The history of this church is somewhat unique. It dates back to the period in which the Catholic religion was persecuted after the Protestant Reform. A rich, devoted Catholic, Boelenz, bought the House of Moses and Aäron at the corner of Jodenbreestraat from a Jewish merchant and converted it into a secret chapel where he reunited companions of the same faith. Over the centuries, the church was enlarged until it reached its present dimensions. It was consecrated only in 1841 after a Belgian architect had built its compact Neoclassic façade with four massive columns crowned by a *statue of Christ*. Two twin towers rise up at the sides of the roof balustrade. The Church of Moses and Aäron ceased to hold religious services some time ago. It is a sort of social centre where yoga courses, concerts, festivals and showmarts are held.

STATUE OF THE DOCK WORKER

It is attributed to Mari Andriessen, but its significance goes beyond its artistic value. It is the statue that Amsterdam dedicated to the dock workers' strike proclaimed in February 1941 against the first deportations of Jews in Germany. The whole city came to a halt following the example of the dockers and even today on the 25th February of every year the inhabitants of Amsterdam gather around this statue in memory of that day.

GERMAN SYNAGOGUE

On the western side of the Jonas Daniel Meijerplein, dedicated to a lawyer who fought strenuously dur-

The monument to the Dock-Worker.

The Church of Moses and Aäron:

> *The German Synagogue, seat of the Jewish Museum.*

The Portuguese Synagogue built during the second half of the 17th century.

ing the French invasion for the Jewish cause, another imposing synagogue occupies a whole corner of the square. It is the complex of the German Synagogue which has housed the new Jewish museum since 1987.

It is an authentic complex comprising four synagogues, two large and two small ones. Its construction was complex and followed the expansion of the Jewish community in Amsterdam; the first synagogue was built in 1670 while the others were built between 1686 and 1752. Since 1955, the German Synagogue has belonged to the Amsterdam Municipality.

PORTUGUESE SYNAGOGUE

The presence of Jews in Holland and in particular in Amsterdam goes back to the second half of the 16th century. As the name of this particular synagogue suggests most of them came frome Portugal. The long and bloody persecution of the Jews throughout the Iberian penin- sula, especially in Spain, had caused the dispersion from the early 15th century on. Some of them had sought an escape by converting to Catholicism, but despite the fact that some of the converts were notorious for their spiteful behaviour towards their brethren, most of these new Catholics, known as Marranos, had secretly kept alive their strong Jewish feeling. During 1481-1495, the Spanish Inquisition enacted still another bitter persecution against the Jews who had found temporary refuge in Portugal. But in 1536 when the Inquisition was instituted in Portugal as well, the Marranos were forced to take flight once more. Luckily, Charles V granted them the right to settle in the Netherlands where, apart from a brief period of persecution instigated by the same Inquistion they were able to benefit from the great tolerance following the Reformation and the success of the Utrecht Union. The converts could thus rid themselves of their falsely acquired Catholicism and return to the faith of their forefathers. Naturally, their origins were reflected in their houses of worship. This synagogue in Amsterdam is one of the most beautiful in the world; the vast building, the southeast facade of which faces toward Jerusalem, was erected between 1671 and 1675 by Elias Bouman and was restored in 1955.

The interior consists of a single large hall, with three wooden barrel-vault ceilings, all the same size and held up by four massive columns of the Ionic order. The Synagogue stands out above the many low buildings around it. In the middle of these is an interesting place, the famous "Est Haim-Livrania D. Montezinos" library, full of books all on the same subject matter, the history of the Spanish and Portuguese Jews, and written for the most part in either Hebrew or Spanish.

The interior of the Synagogue featuring three wooden vaults.

HOUSES
OF AMSTERDAM

All the old houses in the town are distinguished both by their dimensions and their architectural features (specially in the crowning part of the façade which varies in accordance with the building period). High on the gable of these can be seen the projecting beam used as a hoist at the time when the houses' attics served as storerooms. The goods, transported as far as the warehouse-residence by water, were hoisted up to the attic with a winch, consisting of a projecting wooden pole with a pulley and a stout rope reaching down to the ground. The ground floors of many buildings have been turned into shops, the most typical - and interesting - of which are the antique shops. The

On these pages, some examples of the amazing variety and fantasy offered by the copings of Amsterdam's houses. Especially in the facades of the oldest homes, one can sometimes catch a glimpse of the protruding beam used as a hoist at the time of houses-come-storehouses which could be reached by water.

Colourful doors with gilt knobs, barrel-organs, puppet theatres and herring-vendors also form part of the Amsterdam scene.

passion for collecting was part of the Amsterdammer's character from as early as the 16th century. Everybody in Amsterdam collected paintings in the 16th century, from men of letters such as Marten van Papenbroeck and painters like Frans Badens to the burgomasters of the city themselves, including J. Pz. Reael. A century later, Rembrandt himself was to turn collector. The inhabitants of Amsterdam have always decorated their houses with a particular taste; apart from the numerous traditionally embossed tiles, often depicting allegories, homes with scales exist, including an unusual example enriched by a bench, a meeting place for passers-by. More recently, doors have been distinguished by applying unique ranges of objects, like the door featuring tens of bells.

When strolling around in search of these unique houses, it is easy to come across other peculiar aspects of town folklore, such as the crank organ-players (with instruments of all sizes and appearances), guitar-players, the puppeteers with their cloth theatres and the herring-vendors. A typical Dutch snack, herrings are served on the streets in little kiosks and are also eaten while standing up; the "new" herrings, fished between May and September, are a real speciality when served with onions.

JORDAAN

It is the most beautiful district in Amsterdam. And it is the usual paradox: when Jordaan was built in 1600, it was an overpopulated district, a mass of huts one on top of the other. Poverty-stricken craftsmen lived there and the contrast between the wretched houses of Jordaan and the magnificent baroque buildings of the surrounding canals was glaring.

These sad, legendary origins were followed by a present of Bohemian glory: Jordaan is a fashionable district, a favourite haunt of artists, young people and intellectuals.

Jordaan is full of small shops, boutiques, artisan workshops and, above all, Amsterdam's best "bruine cafés", the famous cafés blackened by smoke. During the month of September the streets of Jordaan, as if in a final burst of summer, go mad with the district's festival. The festival lasts ten days with all the streets lit up, outdoor dinners, receptions, dances, exhibitions, processions and a tug-of-war between the two banks of a canal.

BLOEMGRACHT

Bloemgracht, was once known as Jordaan's "Gentlemen's Canal". This was the residential area of the richest craftsmen and therefore contains the most beautiful houses. The traces of this relative prosperity are still evident and this magnificent canal offers many points of interest: at no. 20 one comes across a café exclusively for chessplayers and at no. 38 André Coppenaghen's famous shop, a real supermarket selling little pearls and marbles. At least 1001 qualities are on display in large jars.

EGELANTIERSGRACHT

On Egelantiersgracht, another delightful canal, it is worth mentioning the houses from Nos. 215 to 201, all in the same style; they belonged to the same family as can be seen from the coats-of-arms on the gable. Between Nos. 139 and 107 you will find a charitable institution, Sint Andrieshof.

At the bottom of Egelantiersgracht is to be found a small, famous café, De Smalle, an ideal example of a "bruine café" or café whose walls are blackened by client's smoke. It was here that Peter Hope (famous in Holland for his "jenever", the typical Dutch gin) installed the first alembics of his spirits distillery in 1780.

Characteristic homes on Bloemgracht (no. 97) and Egelantiersgracht (nos. 201-215).

A view of Spiegelgracht; in the background the Rijksmuseum building.

SPIEGELGRACHT

Spiegelgracht is a section of canal that leads from the closed perspective of the Rijksmuseum façade to Nieuwe Spiegelstraat, bordering on the characteristic antique dealers' district.

Probably there is no other place in the world with such an extraordinary concentration of antique shops.

It is a street no longer than 300 metres, but where almost one hundred antique dealers have managed to find space, displaying precious collections, from the rarest such as music boxes to the best-known such as furniture.

LEIDSEGRACHT

Leidsegracht, begun after 1658, is one of the many canals which cross the larger Singel canal and offer so much fascinating scenery. Colourful craft sway gently on the waters, branches of the trees curve down almost touching the canal, creating a play of light among their leaves, and in the background can be seen the tiny bridges.

On these pages some pictures of evocative Leidsegracht, built during the second half of the 17th century.

AMSTERDAM BY NIGHT

When night falls over the town, Amsterdam comes to life. In fact, from the early summer to the early autumn, many canals and monuments are lit up by floodlights and rows of electric-light bulbs to create streams of light that are reflected in the waters. On Herengracht, with its bridge of lit-up arches, the building with the so-called "gemels" stands out; on the Amstel the magnificent sequence of buildings forms a backdrop for Magere Brug, the drawbridge that disappears into the dark thanks to the endless electric-light bulbs that outline it. It is also fascinating at night to look at Munttoren whose lines and series of arches are lit up by electric-light bulbs.

The city after nightfall, when it is lit up by floodlights and rows of electric light bulbs that create phantasmagoric reflections on canals.

Two views of Thorbeckeplein; the former features the statue of the statesman Jan Rudolf Thorbecke.

THORBECKEPLEIN

This square, adjacent to Rembrandtsplein, is called after Jan Rudolf Thorbecke, a famous 19th Century Dutch statesman; creator of the 1848 Constitution, which is still basically in force today, he was an active legislator and during the 60's of the past century he promoted the development of the ports of Amsterdam and Rotterdam thanks to emergency canalization. Known for its bars, rendezvous and restaurants, it overlooks Herengracht where it joins Reguliersgracht, enabling a whole series of effective views over waterways.

The garden of vast Rembrandtsplein.

REMBRANDTS-PLEIN

This large square, filled with cafés, bars and cabarets, is one of the most popular amusement centres in Amsterdam. It was previously known as the Botermarkt, referring to the fact that dairy products and poultry were sold there. In 1876 the statue of Rembrandt, done in 1852 by L. Royer, was erected in the centre of the square, which was given the name it has today.

The square brings us to Reguliersbreestraat, another of Amsterdam's colourful streets. A modern business thoroughfare, it announces the city's gay area: the favourite haunts of the Dutch homosexual community but also the street of the smallest police station in the world, Italian pizzerias, fast-foods and video-games. It is parallel to exclusive Reguliersdwarsstraat, which offers quite the opposite setting. In Reguliersbreestraat, do not fail to take a peep at a rather unusual place for a tourist: a cinema called Tuschinski, which is not just a cine-

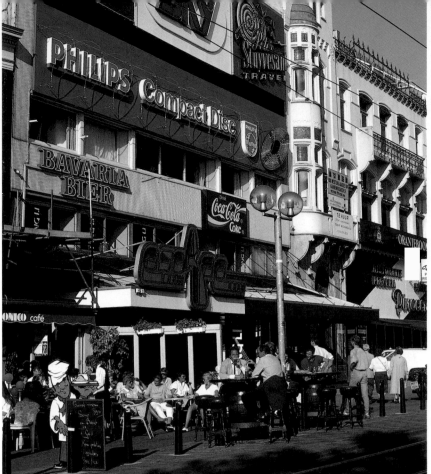

ma but also the deification of art nouveau or the like. Since it was inaugurated in 1921, Tuschinski ha never ceased to fascinate. It was the masterpiece of a great pioneer of the thatre, Abram Icek Tuschinski, a Polish Jew who attended obsessively to every detail of this splendid cinema palace. His *bust,* alongside that of the first owners, Ehrlich and Gerschtanowitz, stands out against a star-studded blue background behind the bar counter. Tuschinski did not escape the Nazis; he died at Auschwitz in 1942, but his cinema-theatre is still one of the most fantastic halls in Europe.

The statue of Rembrandt built in 1852 and placed in the centre of Rembrandtsplein, surrounded by a large number of cafés and bars.

The world's smallest police station on Reguliersbreestraat.

Reguliersbreestraat with the Munttoren in the background.

The Art Nouveau façade of the Tuschinski Cinema (1921).

AMSTEL

It was on the banks of the Amstel that the first settlers founded what was to be the city of Amsterdam, and the names of the streets in this oldest part of the city recall their origins. Running parallel to the Amstel on each side are two large canals, known collectively as the Voorburgwal, a name referring to the wall or moat in front of the city. The older of these is the Oudezijds Voorburgwal and the more recent the Nieuwezijds Voorburgwal, meaning respectively "old side of the wall" and "new side of the wall". The part of the Amstel called the Binnen-Amstel, or Inner Amstel, is perhaps the canal which best displays the beautiful effect of harmony and equilibrium achieved by the combination of the waters and houses of Amsterdam.

Panoramic views of the Kloveniersburgwal and Amstel.

BLAUW BRUG

The Blauw Brug, or Blue Bridge, owes its name to a bridge that no longer exists and which was painted the characteristic blue of the Ductch flag. However, it kept its name also after 1883 when it was replaced by the spans of a new bridge which is none other than an exact copy of the Alexandre Bridge in Paris. It was a strange, architectural decision that did not fail to spark off disputes among the inhabitants of Amsterdam who were not used to the excessive refinement of this new bridge that contrasted with all the others, which were more functional than beautiful.

Blauw Brug, or Blue Bridge, on the Amstel named after the pre-existing bridge painted in the blue of the Dutch flag and demolished in 1880-83.

On these pages views of the Amstel crossed by a characteristic counterposed bridge at the point in which Nieuwe Herengracht flows into it.

MAGERE BRUG

The Blauw Brug clashes with the nearby Magere Brug. It is the most photographed bridge in town. It is the last of the hundreds of wooden bridges that cross Amsterdam's canals. 80 metres long, it is a drawbridge in perpetual movement to allow barges on the Amstel to pass. When it was built, it was just a narrow foot-bridge. It was then widened into a double drawbridge in 1772. Its name is full of ambiguities: Magere is the architect who designed it, but "magere" in Dutch also means thin and its narrow lines are its most distinctive feature. Lastly, two sisters insisted on the first foot-bridge being built over the Amstel; they lived nearby and were naturally called Magere.

Magere Brug on the Amstel, a 80 metre-long wooden counterposed bridge.

THEATER CARRÉ

The Theater Carré gets its name from its builder, Oscar Carré, who had it erected during the past century in the diamond cutters' district. For the traditional circus activity, this member of a well-known Dutch family inaugurated the large white building with its characteristic rounded roof in November 1887. The circus performances held there dwindled with the death of Carré; therefore, at the turn of the century, the theatre was used for recitals, light opera and opera, which it still is.

Three evocative partial views of the Amstel and the Theater Carré, opened in 1887.

BOATS

Every day Amsterdam's waters teem with boats: barges, sailing and rowing boats, motor boats and steamers to tour the city, not to mention kajaks and pedalos for rental to visit canals.

Not all boats are used for transport; some of them are real house-boats, used both by those who enjoy a different kind of accomodation and those who have difficulty in finding an apartment. Barges, full of stray cats, provide an unusual sight.

Boats for all tastes on city canals: from barges to pedaloes.

PRINSENEILAND

In their early trading days, the merchants of Amsterdam used the attics of their own homes as their warehouses. When this was no longer sufficient, they built new structures alongside their homes. But the companies gradually became bigger and bigger, setting up trade ties throughout the world from the Tropics to America and Japan, and warehouses became Amsterdam's most important building. Artificial islands thus had to be built in order to create space for warehouses and storerooms big enough to contain the masses of merchandise which represented the city's strength and life-blood. This island, built on the IJ, owes its name to the so-called House "de Drie Prinsen" (House of the Tree Princes), which had on its wall the busts of three princes of the House of Orange: William I, known as William the Silent, Prince Maurice and Prince Frederick Henry. It is interesting to see the wide facades of the island's warehouses, with their closed shutters, because they still give a sense of the powerful and dynamic role which Amsterdam played in world commerce. Three and a half centuries after they were built, they continue to demonstrate the wisdom and foresight which went into their planning, since most of the warehouses here are still in use today.

THE PORT

Amsterdam, the only city in the world which was born on and has always lived by the water, naturally has a large port, indeed one of the most important in the world today. Until the 17th century large Dutch merchant sailing vessels used to reach the North Sea by sailing through the wide arms of the Zuidersee. The progressive silting up of this vast bay complicated navigation until it risked blocking it. In 1818 a remedy was found by digging the Dutch Channel. But soon this channel proved to be insufficient for the requirements of the large port of Amsterdam. Therefore

Two views of the port and impressive building of the Nederlandse Scheepvaartsmuseum, the Marine Museum.

The old storehouses of Prinseneiland.

a direct channel between the centre of the port and the North Sea was engineered. Work on the North Sea Channel commenced in 1872; 18 metres long, it was completed four years later. At the time it was one of the greatest water works ever constructed. Amsterdam was then once again ready to compete with Rotterdam and reopened its quays to commercial traffic.

The port of Amsterdam and its seaward channel are two huge basins protected against the tides; large shops docking in Amsterdam do not have to resort to harbour tugs. The whole harbour area has been reclaimed from the sea and its quays for a total length of 40 kilometeres are built on artificial islands.

WINDMILLS

The first mention of the windmill at Amsterdam goes back to 1307, and since at least that time the Dutch have used its basically simple mechanism not only to reclaim as much land as possible from the sea but also to grind wheat and saw wood, pump water and process oil, tobacco and cocoa. In a 1765 tax register concerning windmills no less than 140 are mentioned, though of these unfortunately very few remain today. One of the most typical is the Rieker Mill so called from the name of the "polder" (canal) near Amsterdam from which it was transferred in 1956 to its present site in the suburban area of Buitenveldert.

The polder windmill made from wood is the most common one in Holland. Usually it has a base with eight sides, though sometimes with six or twelve. The windmill was adjusted from outside to set the direction of the sails though as mills became more sophisticated some were designed with sails set against the wind automatically.

Some of the windmills that have survived in suburban areas. In 1765 there were at least 140 of them.

CONTENTS